THE PROSPERITY MINDSET

THE CORNERSTONE PUBLISHING

GBENGA SHOWUNMI

THE PROSPERITY MINDSET

Developing the Audacious Mind For Financial Prosperity

ISBN: 978-1-944652-16-6

Published By:

Cornerstone Publishing
A division of Cornerstone Creativity Group LLC
Info@thecornerstonepublishers.com
www.thecornerstonepublishers.com

Author's Information

For speaking engagement or to order books
by Pastor Gbenga Showunmi:
Visit www.gbengashowunmi.com
E-mail: info@gbengashowunmi.com
+1 516-547-4999
Facebook.com/gshowunmi
twitter.com/gshowunmi

CONTENTS

PREFACE

If you had asked me, some years back, if I could ever write a book on a subject as this, my answer would have been a vehement "NO". There was no way I could write on something that I had not experienced myself. Growing up in Africa, Nigeria, to be specific, my family was of lower class. We ate whatever was available, whenever it was available. To put it simply, I was very familiar with poverty.

I started trusting God for a change in my family. In the process, I got saved and accepted Jesus as my Lord and Savior. But then I was misled to believe that money and prosperity belonged to the world. I was taught to have a negative mindset about prosperity. Prosperity for the believer was like a curse, a gift from the devil to drag the believer straight to hell.

With this kind of mentality, it was no surprise that poverty, the opposite of prosperity, continued to dominate our lives. For me, in particular, poverty was a constant companion for many years. I groaned under its weight as it limited me in so many ways. Even the spiritual life that I was taught would be strengthened by poverty became a big struggle because of untold hardship. I had thought this was the perfect will of God for me – until God began to open my eyes to the truths of the Scripture on His real desire for my life as a believer.

The deep revelations I got caused a revolution in my thinking and brought a transformation to my life. It was as if a blindfold was removed from my eyes and the pathway to heavenly abundance opened right before me. From then on, my family and I have never ceased to enjoy uncommon financial breakthroughs.

What you have in this book is a collection of some of the liberating secrets I discovered about prosperity as I searched the Scriptures and interacted with some notable men of God.

Many believers today are shackled by the yokes of poverty and burdened by debts, not because they have been destined to be so, or that God is happy with their state, but because they have conditioned their minds to accept financial hardship as their portion in life. As far as they are concerned, even though the death of Christ was meant to destroy the works of the devil in their lives – these works only involve sin and sickness, not poverty. In fact, some have gone to the extent of seeing wretched living as a badge of true Christianity. And as they wallow in the slumber of ignorance, Satan continues to rejoice in their shame and limitations, while his own children continue to populate hell with the massive resources at their disposal.

THE PROSPERITY MINDSET is a revolutionary call to all believers to wake up from our self-inflicted slumber of substandard living and embrace the full package of glorious benefits that Christ has purchased for us with His blood. We have slept for too long, under the influence of doctrinal errors and fallacies – and thus left Satan to wreak havoc on our lives and churches. What Christ has come to give us is abundant life – a life that knows no lack or limitation in any area of our lives. Until we accept this truth, we may continue to languish in lack while unbelievers around us continue to enjoy the riches created and owned by our Father.

The central message of this book is indeed timely and eye-opening. God cannot transform our situations if we are not ready to renew our minds. We can never become prosperous while we harbor and cherish the mentality of a pauper. The emancipating revelations in this book will jolt you to see the abundant riches that belong to you, as well as propel you to take your rightful position as an heir of God's Kingdom. Every chapter contains life-changing truths and yoke breaking declarations. Get set for a mental repositioning that will launch you to the realm of the prosperous!

Gbenga Showunmi
Houston, Texas

CHAPTER 1

GOD WANTS YOU TO PROSPER

"Beloved, I pray that you may prosper in all things and be in health, just as your soul prospers" (3 John 2).

This perhaps is the most exciting news you'll ever hear in your life. To someone who probably has experienced or witnessed so much poverty, debt-burdens and substandard living, this may sound unbelievable and indeed unimaginable. But the truth, as this Scripture reveals, is that more than anything else in the world, the Almighty God who created you wants you to prosper in all things and enjoy fullness of life.

To "prosper" according to the dictionary, is to be "successful, flourishing, or be in thriving condition in financial or good fortune". This is God's desire for your life. In His plan for your life and destiny, poverty is an anomaly. In fact, in His original plan for the whole of humanity, poverty wasn't even a consideration; it's a complete aberration.

Has it ever occurred to you that it was not a mere coincidence that man was the last of God's creations? Or let me put it this way – have you ever wondered why God created man last? There was a grand purpose in that – and that was to ensure that the man that would be created would live in abundance. He was not to lack anything. This was why he was placed in the Garden of Eden – a garden that was garnished with opulence and brimming with abundance of luxuries and resources.

Here is how the Scripture describes the place God placed the first man – the place He intends all of His children to be:

"The Lord God planted a garden eastward in Eden, and there He put the man whom He had formed. And out of the ground the Lord God made every tree grow that is pleasant to the sight and good for food…Now a river went out of Eden to water the garden, and from there it parted and became four riverheads…And the gold of that land is good. Bdellium and the onyx stone are there." (Genesis 2:8-12).

Did you notice the last part in particular – where it says that not only did God place the man in a land filled with gold but that the gold is GOOD, meaning it was a special one. And added to the gold were other precious stones. That was God's picture and purpose for man – a beautiful reflection of His own abode in heaven.

It was the entrance of sin into the world that brought poverty and other ills that we see all around us today. Man, in transgression of God's instruction, gave in to the lies of Satan and became exposed to his ravaging works. For "the thief does not come except to steal, and to kill, and to destroy…" (John 10:10). Cheeringly however, as our introductory reference and many other Scripture references show, man's unfaithfulness has never and can never alter God's faithfulness. That man strayed by violating God's word does not alter the original purpose of God for His own. This is why God continues to desire and ensure the fulfillment of His original purpose of prosperity in the lives of His children.

Let me briefly show you this perpetual desire of God for your prosperity with Scripture references, as well as some personalities in which the desire was actualized.

SCRIPTURAL TRUTH

- **Deuteronomy 8:18** - And you shall remember the Lord your God, for it is He who gives you power to get wealth…

- **Deuteronomy 28:12** - The Lord will open to you His good treasure, the heavens, to give the rain to your land in its season, and to bless all the work of your hand. You shall lend to many nations, but you shall not borrow.

- **1 Samuel 2:8** - He raises the poor from the dust and lifts the beggar from the ash heap, to set them among princes and make them inherit the throne of glory.

- **Job 36:11** - If they obey and serve Him, They shall spend their days in prosperity, and their years in pleasures.

- **Psalm 34:10** - The young lions lack and suffer hunger; But those who seek the Lord shall not lack any good thing.

- **Psalm 35:27** …Let the Lord be magnified, Who has pleasure in the prosperity of His servant.

- **Psalms 112:2-3:** "…The generation of the upright will be blessed. Wealth and riches will be in his house, And his righteousness endures forever."

- **Proverbs 10:22:** The blessing of the Lord makes one rich, and He adds no sorrow with it.

- **Malachi 3:10:** Bring all the tithes into the storehouse, That there may be food in My house, and try Me now in this," Says the Lord of hosts, "If I will not open for you the windows of heaven and pour out for you such blessingThat there will not be room enough to receive it.

- **2 Corinthians 8:9:** For you know the grace of our Lord Jesus Christ, that though He was rich, yet for your sakes He became poor, that you through His poverty might become rich.

- **Philippians 4:19:** And my God shall supply all your need according to His riches in glory by Christ Jesus.

There are several other scripture passages that emphasize the delight of God in your prosperity, but I believe the revelations from the above passages should provide sufficient illumination into God's purpose for you. They should serve to convince you that it is not God's will that you accept poverty as a normal way of life.

However beyond the promises and declarations on prosperity in the Scripture, there is also the vital need to see if there were visible manifestations in the lives of the people of God. Are these promises realistic or are they exaggerated? Could it be possible, as the above scriptures point out, for a child of God to be plenteous in goods, to never be in debt, to have bank-bursting wealth, to have abundance of gold and silver, to spend every day in prosperity, to have every need of one's life supplied and never be in want? Let's look at the some individuals in the scripture to ascertain this.

Abraham

The Scripture says of Abraham that he "was very rich in livestock, in silver, and in gold" (Genesis 13:2). That man obeyed the call of God to come out of his idolatrous background (which we may refer to today as being saved) and from then on, God's blessings upon his life were without measure. He was so successful and prosperous in all his endeavors that he became a wonder to many. His servant once testified of him: "The Lord has blessed my master greatly, and he has become great; and He has given him flocks and herds, silver and gold, male and female servants, and camels and donkeys." (Genesis 24:35).

God also made reference to Abraham while showing the Israelites what He could do for them if they served Him faithfully. God told them, "Look unto Abraham your father…for I called him alone, and blessed him, and increased him" (Isaiah 51:2). It is my belief that for God to be using Abraham as a model of his blessing it means that He wants us to be as blessed as Abraham was. And indeed, the provision has been made for this to happen. I will be showing this to you later on.

Isaac

Genesis 26:12-14 says of Isaac, "Then Isaac sowed in that land, and received in the same year an hundredfold: and the LORD blessed him. And the man waxed great, and went forward, and grew until he became very great: For he had possession of flocks, and possession of herds, and great store of servants: and the Philistines envied him."

God so prospered Isaac that he became a source of envy to those around him. But that aside, I want you to observe two important things from the Scripture verse. First, is the emphasis on "that land" and "same year". Those two expressions have significance for every true child of God. The reference to the land was necessary because the said land was supposed to be barren as at that time. It was a time of great famine when the land produced little or nothing. Yet Isaac sowed and reaped bountiful, hundredfold harvest – which means that he prospered where many saw nothing but hunger, he flourished where many were perishing and he succeeded where many were failing. Also, "that year" when his riches began to be extremely pronounced was a year that many considered extremely difficult and challenging. The economy of the nation was in shambles – but that became the beginning of the best season of Isaac's life.

The second thing is the scope of his prosperity. It was both extensive and progressive. It kept increasing and in fact multiplying. He "waxed great and went forward, until he became very great". What power was upon Isaac that made him immune to general distress and nation-wide downturn? It was the power of prosperity from the Almighty God.

Jacob

The Bible records concerning Jacob that not only was he prosperous but he was EXCEEDINGLY so. "Thus the man became exceedingly prosperous, and had large flocks, female and male servants, and camels and donkeys." (Genesis 30:43).

In case you don't know, another word for exceedingly is EXTRAORDINARILY – which means that Jacob's wealth was explosive by all means. Even his brother, Esau, who did not receive as much blessing as him from their father, equally lived a life of riches and abundance. Both of them were so rich that they were forced to go apart. "Then Esau took his wives, his sons, his daughters, and all the persons of his household, his cattle and all his animals, and all his goods which he had gained in the land of Canaan, and went to a country away from the presence of his brother Jacob. For their possessions were too great for them to dwell together, and the land where they were strangers could not support them because of their livestock." (Genesis 36:6-7).

What great prosperity did these people enjoy! Their wealth was bursting, overflowing, so much that the land could not contain their combined wealth. And what stops you from having same today?

David

Concerning David, the Bible tells us that "he died in a good old age, full of days and riches and honor; and Solomon his son reigned in his place." (1 Chronicles 29:28). Did you read that? HE WAS FULL OF RICHES! The man was so familiar with prosperity that he testified, "I have been young, and now am old; Yet I have not seen the righteous forsaken, Nor his descendants begging bread" (Psalms 37:25). Again, I ask, what makes the cases of many believers different today? Why are many living from hand to mouth and many more in debts? Could God have changed or could it be that we no longer know our rights and privileges? We know that God is unchanging; therefore the problem must be with us!

Solomon

It was God Himself that promised to bless Solomon with prosperity after his prayer for wisdom. In 2 Chronicles 1:12, God told him: "I will give you riches and wealth and honor, such as none of the kings have had who were before you, nor shall any after you have the like." And did He fulfill the promise? Of course, God never lies! The same 2 Chronicles later records that "All King Solomon's drinking vessels were gold, and all the vessels of the House of the Forest of Lebanon were pure gold. Not one was silver…So King Solomon surpassed all the kings of the earth in riches and wisdom." (9:20-22).

Did you observe the different time frames between all these people I have mentioned? Yet God keeps demonstrating his faithfulness to His promises and willingness to prosper His people. Let's proceed to the New Testament to see a few more examples.

Joseph of Arimathea

Here was a man described as a disciple of Jesus Christ, and yet God blessed him with physical riches as well. Matthew 27:57 says, "Now when evening had come, there came a rich man from Arimathea, named Joseph, who himself had also become a disciple of Jesus. This man went to Pilate and asked for the body of Jesus. Then Pilate commanded the body to be given to him." Now you see it clearly from the Scripture – being a committed disciple of Christ does not automatically confer the yoke of poverty on you!

Female Supporters Of Christ

These included Joanna, Susanna and many other women of substance who were prosperous enough to continually support the ministry of Jesus Christ. "Now it came to pass, afterward, that He went through every city and village, preaching and bringing the glad tidings of the kingdom of God. And the twelve were with Him, and certain women who had been healed of evil spirits and infirmities—Mary called Magdalene, out of whom had come seven demons, and Joanna the wife of Chuza, Herod's steward, and Susanna, and many others who provided for Him from their substance." (Luke 8:1-3)

Cornelius the Centurion

Cornelius was described as a devout and God-fearing man, who obviously was very rich as he was known to be committed to acts of charity. He was not only said to be given to giving alms but giving it GENEROUSLY. "There was a certain man in Caesarea called Cornelius, a centurion of what was called the Italian Regiment, a devout man and one who feared God with all his household, who gave alms generously to the people, and prayed to God always" (Acts 10:1-2).

As I said before, there are several other examples I could have cited but that's not my intention here. What I want to show you is that God is no respecter of persons. His desire for these people that made them prosper is also His desire for you. It is up to you then to vehemently reject poverty. It is a contradiction of God's will for your life.

CHAPTER 2

FALSE PERCEPTIONS ON PROSPERITY

One of the strategies that Satan has perpetually used to rob believers of their birthrights in Christ is to blindfold them with false perceptions. And it appears that where this is most pronounced is in the subjects of prosperity and poverty. There are entrenched perceptions that people have in these areas that are at best impoverishing and at worst unscriptural. I regret to say that I myself had once held these beliefs as influenced by my upbringing.

However, before clarifying the false perceptions, let me first establish one fact that forms the focus of this book and equally has scriptural foundation: Our perceptions about life in general influence our attitudes and actions. As a man thinks in his heart, so is he. Sometimes we think that there is a problem with our environment or the particular object we are looking at, not knowing that the real issue is with our eyesight. This is called the theory of selective perception, which states that people tend to perceive things according to their inherent beliefs more than as the objects of focus really are, and react accordingly.

This explanation is apt for the subject of prosperity. The reason many believers are poor today is not because God doesn't want to prosper them but because they see prosperity as evil. This is why apart from being challenged by the examples and scripture passages I showed you in chapter one, another thing I pray to be accomplished in your life is the uprooting of misconceptions about poverty and prosperity. Let me explain it this way.

PROSPERITY IS NOT A SIN

That the most holy God Himself is the one who is desiring that you should be rich and prosperous shows that there is nothing wrong in prosperity. It is part of your fundamental rights as a child of God. The Bible says, "He who did not spare His own Son, but delivered Him up for us all, how shall He not with Him also freely give us all things?" (Romans 8:32).

Let's get this straight. It is not a sin to be rich – God

Himself is rich. If being rich is something evil, the Scripture wouldn't have said, "In the day of prosperity be joyful…" (Ecclesiastes 7:1). What God condemns however is greedily coveting after riches by using worldly tactics (see Paul's warning in 1 Timothy 6:10); trusting in riches to the neglect of God and detriment of the soul (as in the case of the Rich Fool, Luke 12:13-21); and being selfish with riches (as in the case of the story of the Rich Man and Lazarus, Luke 16:19-31).

So, you can be rich and still serve God wholeheartedly. You can be rich and still make it to heaven. The key is having the right attitude towards money and prosperity. The secret lies in always acknowledging God as the source of our riches, fulfilling the responsibilities automatically conferred on us as soon as we're blessed and keeping our affection above and not on earth. It's all a matter of grace. Many people like Abraham who were blessed with abundant riches still served God without distractions. How much more now that the grace of God is abundantly available to us!

Here's Paul's timeless admonition to Christians blessed with riches: "Command those who are rich in this present age not to be haughty, nor to trust in uncertain riches but in the living God, who gives us richly all things to enjoy" (1 Timothy 6:17). Did you observe that Paul himself admits that it's possible to be rich in money and rich in faith? Did you observe that he never said those who are rich in this world are sinners and candidates of hell? Good. He even goes ahead to emphasize that it is God who richly gives us all things to enjoy, including prosperity. Why then should we shackle ourselves with the yoke of poverty?

In the next chapter, I'll be providing more reasons on why prosperity in itself is not a sin by explaining in details why God wants you to prosper.

POVERTY IS NOT PIETY

This is a crucial point you must note. Poverty is never a short-cut to God's Kingdom. It is not synonymous with righteousness. In fact, as we shall be considering in the next chapter, poverty can even be a barrier to a robust relationship with God. No wonder the wise man prayed against poverty in the Bible, saying, "lest I be poor and steal, and profane the name of my God." (Proverbs 30:9).

What this means is that neither the rich nor the poor is immune to sinning. Both poverty and prosperity come with their peculiar temptations – just as the rich is faced with the temptation of being carried away by the privileges of riches, so also is the poor prone to the temptation of being led astray by the frustrations of poverty. So, why stay poor in the name of wanting to be closer to God?

Again contrary to what many think, poverty is not always humbling. There are many poor people who are prouder than a peacock and bitter than a serpent. In their poverty, they are so haughty and so bitter towards others, especially the rich. To them, all rich people are vain, vacuous and vicious people who must have obtained their riches by dishonesty. How this reflects righteousness or humility is unclear to me. In fact, I like the way a Christian writer explained this:

"The Bible tells us to be humble. Many believe that being humble, means driving a rust bucket and eating mac and cheese for dinner every night. They think that because they don't eat of the good of the land, that they are more spiritual than those who do. Poverty is poverty, and has nothing to do with humility! Some in the body of Christ are even proud of their poorness, and that is nothing more than religious pride. That is the exact opposite of true humility! Others look at some of God's wealthy ministers and scoff saying that they have too much money. I wonder how they would treat Abraham if he lived in this day and age? Perhaps Job, who was extremely wealthy? Or Solomon? Or Lot, who was told to leave the country because of his great wealth?"

Pastor Kenneth Hagin also shared his own experience: "For many years I did not understand that it is God's will for His children to prosper. I thought as many do that poverty was a characteristic of humility – that in order to be humble one must be poor. I thought that a righteous man could not be wealthy and that a wealthy man could not be righteous. Any promise in the scriptures regarding financial blessing applied only to the Jews, I thought. I have since learned, through studying God's Word and applying it in my own life, that God wants His children to "prosper and be in health, even as thy soul prospereth"

PROSPERITY IS NOT A NEW GOSPEL

There is one claim that is becoming increasingly popular, especially among conservative Christians. Whether in their gatherings, publications, multi-media messages or online posts, the argument remains the same – that teachings on financial and material prosperity for the righteous are devilish and part of the last days strategies of the forces of darkness to distract believers from heaven. This is nothing but a misleading and unscriptural argument.

To begin with, I'm not going to deny that there are false preachers today, "whose god is their belly… who set their mind on earthly things" (Philippians

3:19). Yes, there are many who go to the extreme by focusing only on earthly blessings and prosperity, while neglecting or relegating the fundamental requirements of righteousness and godliness in all things. These are people who focus on pampering the flesh while the soul suffers; people who seem to ignore the commandment to "seek first the Kingdom of God and His righteousness" (Matthew 6:33).

I admit that this approach is damnable. But the question is: do we deal with an error with another error? Do we tackle one extreme by going to another extreme? No way. The fact that certain people abuse the provision and promise of prosperity for God's people doesn't mean that prosperity is a sin, or that God doesn't want His people to prosper anymore. Nor does it remove God's promises of prosperity from the Scripture. So what do we do? Simple. We learn to balance things up – not pretending or denying God's words! Otherwise we make God to be a liar and His words misleading.

Honestly, I'm baffled about what seems to have become widespread obsession with attacking the message of prosperity. Why is this aspect of redemption being constantly discredited? So many preachers have abused and continued to abuse the provisions of healing and deliverance today, especially in places like Africa where lots of these people perform some abracadabra to deceive the gullible. But does it mean that healing and deliverance are out of place in God's Kingdom? Does this make healing sinful or deliverance evil? Does it make it necessary to condemn or deny God's promises and provisions for our healing? Not at all. Many Christians continue to trust God for healing deliverance, citing Scriptural promises and examples – both in the Old and New Testaments to claim that it is their right. So, I ask – how is this different from seeking prosperity?

I think we are simply allowing Satan to cheat us by claiming just one portion of our inheritance and looking away from another. And not only that – we are actually claiming that the other part is from Satan and not from God. No wonder many Christians are suffering ignorantly today and no wonder God Himself said, "My people perish for lack of knowledge".

Now, on the issue of whether prosperity preaching is a new phenomenon among modern day preachers, let me emphasize that this is equally. Again let me reiterate that while there's definitely a surge in proliferation, frequency and intensity of prosperity preachers in this century, the revelation of God's willingness to prosper his people has always been obtained and propagated, even from the most conservative of puritan Christians.

Let me quickly show you a few of them.

A.W. Pink, who was not a modern day preacher, once said in his January 1944 sermon, A Prosperous New Year:

"Prosperity or the absence of it is not a matter of chance thing, nor is it the product of a blind and inexorable fate. If we do not enjoy prosperity, the fault is entirely our own, and we are dishonest if we ascribe it solely unto the sovereignty of God. "In repentance and rest is your salvation, in quietness and trust is your strength, but you would have none of it" (Isaiah 30:15). Would it not have been flagrantly dishonest, if they attributed their disquietude and fears, to the sovereign will of God? "O that you had hearkened to My commandments! then had your peace been as a river" (Isaiah 48:18), then how wicked to charge God with being responsible for their lack of peace."

What he was saying is simple – prosperity or poverty is a matter of choice, not divine imposition. If, despite all the promises God has given on prosperity, believers refuse to accept and claim their right to be prosperous, it will be both dishonest and wicked to claim that it is God's will for them.

Much earlier before the remark by A.W. Pink, John Angell James too – who was known for his staunch stance on godly living in all his teachings - said in his 1837 sermon, The Christian in Prosperity:

"God should not only be acknowledged—but praised for the blessing of prosperity. It is a blessing, unless by our abuse of it we turn it into a curse; and is spoken of as such throughout the word of God. God has not confounded the distinction between plenty and poverty; nor required us to do so. Prosperity is indeed a mercy, and should be received as such—to be released from privation, and care, and necessity. The man who talks of poverty as a good in itself, speaks alike against reason and against Scriptural revelation. Poverty may be overruled for good, and often is—but in itself it is an evil. A cause of thankfulness it certainly is, to have the comforts of this life… Wealth justly obtained, and piously spent, instead of a curse is a blessing; instead of diminishing a man's religion, increases it; and instead of hindering him in his way to heaven, helps him. Where Providence has blessed you with the possession of wealth, seek for divine grace, that you may be blessed in the use of it, for, without the latter, the former is no blessing at all."

I need not expound on what J.A James has said, since it is simply a reflection of all I had pointed out previously. Let me just reiterate one point he made, proofs of which I'll be showing you in the next chapter – that prosperity, when properly used, can even boost your chances of getting to heaven more easily. And he minced no words in denouncing poverty as an evil because it is unnatural.

Lastly, here is what James Buchanan, in his 1840 sermon, titled Consideration and based on Ecclesiastes 7:14, said:

"There is no such thing in the Bible as a disparagement of what is naturally good, or a recommendation of what is naturally evil…we are nowhere taught to reverse the dictates of nature so as to regard prosperity in itself as evil; or adversity as in itself good. On the contrary, prosperity is declared to be a proper source of joy, and a strong motive for gratitude. While adversity is described as, for the present, not joyous but grievous. And accordingly, the duties which are peculiarly appropriate to each, and the exercises which they respectively require, are stated in express terms, and illustrated by beautiful examples. In prosperity, a cheerful gratitude, a bountiful charity, and self-denial, devoting all of God's gifts to his glory and the good of our fellow-men. In adversity, a resigned and submissive spirit, meek contentment, combined, not with an anxious care — but with a serious thoughtfulness, and a considerate regard of God's dealings towards us, such as may best qualify us for reaping the fruits of affliction, and enjoying religious comforts under its heaviest pressure.

THE RICH MAN AND LAZARUS

Let me quickly use this opportunity to clarify the story of Lazarus and the Rich Man. As I said before, the Rich Man was not condemned because he was rich. He was condemned because he was selfish and godless with his riches. Similarly, Lazarus did not go to heaven because he was poor. It was simply because he revered God in his poverty. If he had been poor and nursed pride, bitterness or envy in him, he still would have continued his suffering in hell. And to show that the rich man was a necessity on earth, wasn't it at his table that Lazarus was longing to eat crumbs? If he were to be poor as Lazarus, who would have to be depended upon to feed the other?

So, let's get our focus clear. Righteousness comes neither by poverty nor by prosperity but by faith in the Son of God, Jesus Christ. As the Scripture says, "But food does not commend us to God; for neither if we eat are we the better, nor if we do not eat are we the worse" (1 Corinthians 8:8). So choose to eat – to eat in the prosperity and abundance that God has provided for you!

CHAPTER 3

WHY GOD WANTS YOU TO PROSPER

Having established, with relevant Scripture references and examples, that prosperity is God's desire for His children, the question naturally comes – Why should God earnestly desire prosperity for me?

There are three broad reasons why God desires that you prosper. One, is because poverty brings limitations. And God doesn't want you to be limited in any area of life. Christ says, "I have come that they may have life, and that they may have it more abundantly." (John 10:10). Two, prosperity brings glory to God. And three, prosperity empowers the believer and the Church of God to fulfill their purposes more easily and effectively.

Let's look at these points in detail.

THE LIMITATIONS OF POVERTY

Poverty is a curse. It was part of the limitations that came as a result of sin. In fact, whenever I read about the effect of poverty from the scripture, I develop holy anger in me. Let me show you some of them.

1. **Poverty causes shame, reproach and stigmatization.** "Wealth makes many friends, but the poor is separated from his friend." (Proverbs 19:4). Who wants to associate with a perpetual beggar and borrower since they know that he has nothing much to offer apart from parasitically feeding on others?

2. **Poverty exposes one to unnecessary health risks, as well as other dangers and calamities**. "The rich man's wealth is his strong city; the destruction of the poor is their poverty. (Proverbs 10:15). How many people have died prematurely or even maimed for life – simply because they cannot afford basic necessities of life? Even more heartbreaking is that many are currently battling with life-limiting ailments that could have easily been treated if they had been financially buoyant. Can God wish this kind of life for anyone? No way!

I think we should at this juncture look at the example of Lazarus in the Bible again. We are told that he was filled with sores that dogs came to lick. His health was in very bad shape and he was exposed to further health risks because of starvation and having his sores exposed without quality health care. The rich man on the other hand had no such sores. What was the difference? Their financial conditions. The rich man fed well and consequently had a healthy life. As I mentioned before, the rich man went to hell – not because he enjoyed a good life but because he had a decadent heart. God wants us to have quality life but this can never be possible in poverty – for "the destruction of the poor is their poverty".

3. Poverty brings humiliation, subjugation and enslavement. "The rich rules over the poor, and the borrower is servant to the lender." (Proverbs 22:7). A classic but very pathetic example of this is found in 2 Kings 4, where a deceased prophet's children were to be enslaved because their father died a debtor. It was the miraculous intervention of Elisha that eventually saved the situation. Can you imagine the extent of humiliation this must have caused for the late prophet's wife who had to run to Elisha, as well as her two children who were being threatened with slavery? Poverty, indeed, is a terrible curse that nobody should live with!

4. Poverty robs one of honor, respect and recognition, even when one deserves them. Ecclesiastes 9:14-16 tells this sad tale of the reproach of poverty: "There was a little city with few men in it; and a great king came against it, besieged it, and built great snares around it. Now there was found in it a poor wise man, and he by his wisdom delivered the city. Yet no one remembered that same poor man. Then I said: "Wisdom is better than strength. Nevertheless the poor man's wisdom is despised, And his words are not heard.""

This is one of the most painful calamities of poverty. Many people have potentials for greatness; many have great business ideas and strategies - but poverty renders them helpless, limited and unknown.

So, how could God wish any of the above for any of His children? It's impossible. "For I know the thoughts that I think toward you, says the Lord, thoughts of peace and not of evil…" (Jeremiah 29:11).

THE GLORY OF PROSPERITY

God delights in your prosperity because your prosperity reflects His nature and brings glory to Him. Let me briefly explain this with a story. Seven years ago, when my wife was pregnant with our first son, it was time to go shopping for the baby's stuff. We were checking out all the items and their prices. I was always inclined to purchase the most expensive and consequently the best stuff in the store. And that was exactly what I did! Why? I wanted the best for my son. It is my joy. I am delighted when I don't have to be ashamed to present my son to the world. I wanted everyone who saw what he wore to acknowledge me for the quality of materials he had.

The prosperity of the father must reflect on his children. If you want to know how prosperous a father is, look at his children. Your children are the reflector of your wealth, as well as who you are. What kinds of food do your children eat? What brands of shoes and clothes do they wear? What sort of schools do they attend? Look at them. A responsible father will display his wealth through his children.

It's the same manner that we human beings want the best for our children that God also want the best for us. In fact, He exceeds us by far in doting on His children! "If you then, being evil, know how to give good gifts to your children, how much more will your Father who is in heaven give good things to those who ask Him!" (Matthew 7:11).

Your life glorifies God when you are financially

strong—when you don't have to beg or borrow to live; when you have enough to spend and to share; when you have no financial or material lack that is limiting you from fulfilling His purpose for you.

What impression does it give concerning God, if despite being the creator and controller of the universe with all its abundant riches, His own children are living in lack and want? Or maybe I should give you a few human illustrations to get a better picture of what I'm saying here – and to make you see why anything short of prosperity for a child of God is an abnormality that should be passionately rejected.

What would you say of a popular president, monarch, business tycoon or multibillionaire whose children are living in poverty and deprivation? What would you say of a renowned fashion designer whose children are constantly in rags? What would you say of a billionaire entrepreneur who controls several chains of businesses but has many jobless children roaming the streets in search of a job? Or of a massive investor in real estates, whose children are among the homeless on the street? Of course I know you would be outraged that such a thing could be happening. In fact, I'm sure you won't even believe it because it would have sounded like an impossibility.

But hasn't it occurred to you that a child of God living in poverty is even in a more disturbing condition? If human beings in wealth and authority wouldn't want their children living in squalid conditions, how much more the righteous God? Humans cannot be more responsible or protective of their reputation and integrity than God. If humans with their limitations would not want anything that will tarnish their image and glory, how much more God, of whom the Scripture says, "The earth is the Lord's, and all its fullness" (Psalms 24:1)?

God does not need the prosperity of earth in heaven. Heaven in itself is a display of wealth created by the extremely rich Father. The streets of heaven are paved with pure gold. I always lightheartedly say that you must acquaint yourself with wealth here on earth so as not to pass out when you find yourself within the vast splendor and magnificence. Many people will indeed be shocked by the majestic opulence of the Kingdom! No wonder Jesus prayed for God's Kingdom to be manifested on earth. God's heavenly Kingdom blossoms in holiness and abundance. And it is His plan that we experience heaven on earth. So, if you are not experiencing heaven on earth, you are living below your calling!

What makes your prosperity even more glorifying to

God is that your prosperity is a confirmation of His faithfulness to His numerous promises of prosperity for His children. If despite His numerous promises of abundance, His children are living in penury, what does it tell us of His integrity and dependability? No wonder then that the Psalmist says, "Let the LORD be magnified, who has pleasure in the prosperity of His servant." (Psalms 35:27).

Yes, God has pleasure in your prosperity! As a believer, your main mandate is to bring pleasure to God. This is something Satan would never want to see happen. Each time you complain of being poor and broke, you are bringing shame to the name God and what excites Satan better than the name of God being despised? The reason Satan wages war against the finances of believers is to hinder them from fulfilling God's purpose for their lives. But you can decide never to allow this be your portion. You were formed for God's glory and you must resist and reject anything that threatens to make you live below this expectation!

THE EMPOWERMENT OF PROSPERITY

Yes, prosperity is empowering – both for the individual believer and the church of God as a whole.

And this is one reason why prosperity is God's delight. With prosperity, anxiety is banished, several barriers and limitations are removed and burdens of debts (with the associated frustrations and shame) and lack become history.

Let me begin with the individual believer. Apart from empowering him to satisfactorily take care of all personal needs without worrying, begging or borrowing, living in prosperity enables the individual to carry out several assignments that God expects of him – giving alms, helping the needy, fulfilling obligations to the government and society, and most importantly contributing to the expansion of God's kingdom through giving and convincing sinners of God's goodness.

Let me take time to elaborate on these points with Scriptural examples. One of the fundamental expectations of God from believers is helping the needy all around us. "Pure and undefiled religion before God and the Father is this: to visit orphans and widows in their trouble…." (James 1:27). Of what use will our visits be to the fatherless and the widows if we can't help to meet their financial needs and alleviate their daily burdens? Of course, many people in poverty don't even bother about fulfilling this requirement of pure religion because they know how embarrassing it will be for them and how frustrating it'll be for their hosts if after visiting and observing key areas of need, they are incapable of helping to meet such needs. The reason Cornelius was noted for giving lots of alms to the needy was because he had the finances to do so.

Now cast your mind to Jesus and his disciples and imagine what would have happened to their ministry if they had found it difficult to pay taxes as required by the government (Matthew 17:24-27). That would have dealt a terrible blow to the message He was to preach later on giving to Caesar what belongs to Caesar (Matthew 22:20-22).

Now, imagine a Christian who can't pay his bills or rent and is being constantly harassed by the authorities. What sort of testimony or reputation would such have? What message of hope can he preach to his landlord or co-tenants? And how can such be focused on serving God when his mind is constantly in turmoil? God wants to us to prosper so we can "serve Him without fear, in holiness and righteousness before Him all the days of our life" (Luke 1:74-75).

But the most important reason God wants you to prosper is because your prosperity is necessary for the advancement and expansion of His Kingdom. This happens, first of all, through the magnetism of the glory of God upon your life. When you're enjoying abundant life – a life that is visibly blessed and is a blessing to others – people naturally want to be associated with you and your God. Who wants to serve a God who seems to delight in impoverishing His children? In the story of the Rich Man and Lazarus – what kind of sermon do you think Lazarus could have given the Rich Man that would have been effective? A sermon that would appear to be inviting him to leave a life of health and enjoyment to a life of perpetual sickness and poverty? Let's be realistic – who wants to listen to such a sermon? Isn't the gospel of Christ supposed to be GOOD NEWS?

The second way your prosperity helps God's kingdom is in your direct financial contribution to the progress of God's work. The Scripture says in 2 Corinthians 9:8, "And God is able to make all grace abound toward you, that you, always having all sufficiency in all things, may have an abundance for every good work." Someone has noted that the word "abound" translates from a Greek word which means "abundance", "more than enough", "to make extremely rich or wealthy" and "to overflow" – which is what God wants for you so that the overflow of His blessings in your life can propel the course of the gospel.

I mentioned it above how some women of substance

constantly ministered to the needs of Christ and His disciples. They were blessed and thus were able to bless the gospel work with their resources. The woman of Shunem and her husband were prosperous and this helped to alleviate the burdens of Elisha (2 Kings 4:8-37). Joseph of Arimathea was prosperous and that helped in giving a befitting burial to our Lord Jesus Christ. What about the Roman centurion who freely paid for the building of a synagogue for the people of God (Romans 7:1-5)? And if Lydia and her household were not prosperous, how would it have been possible to lay the foundation for the first church in Europe which began right in her home (Acts 16:40)!

Now, to the church of God. God knows that without prosperity, a church will certainly be limited in its outreaches and impact. A church enveloped in poverty may languish for long in obscurity. Do you know how many churches and ministers of God today have the WORD but not the wherewithal to publicise it? Their voices are hardly heard because the power of their ministrations is being confined by the shackles of poverty.

Satan understands the havoc the church of God will cause to his kingdom if believers are prospered. This is why he keeps us ignorant of our right to prosperity. Zechariah 1:17 says, "Again proclaim, saying, 'thus says the LORD of hosts: "My cities shall again spread out through prosperity; The LORD will again comfort Zion, And will again choose Jerusalem."

You've seen it right there. Through prosperity will the message of the Kingdom spread out to the ends of the earth. I'm sometimes baffled by the lackadaisical approach of many end-time believers towards financial prosperity. Agents of darkness and wickedness often invest lots of money to spread their messages of evil and depravity through the media and other channels. They invest heavily because their master, the devil, knows the worth of a soul. However, the only counter-attack the church seems to launching is through prayer. We pray for anything, including those things that do not need prayers. No wonder Jesus Himself said "the sons of this world are more shrewd in their generation than the sons of light" (Luke 16:8). We really need to wake up from our slumber if we must win the battle for the spread and domination of the message of the gospel in this end time.

See, prayer is good, and I'm not disputing that. In fact, my first book was on prayer. It was titled "Prophetic Prayer for Divine Intervention." After that I have written three other books on prayer. Some of my friends even call me "Apostle of Prophetic Prayer". So I am a big believer in prayer. But prayer is not a substitute for the function of money. Unfortunately, believers are always behind in understanding their kingdom responsibility. We are to preach the gospel, and money is required to get it done, period!

King Solomon, the richest man in the Bible revealed the power and influence of money in his own words, "...but money answers everything" (Ecclesiastes 10:19). We will reach more people for Christ if we have more kingdom-minded people who will see the subject of prosperity as a necessity in the fight for the souls of men and not just about greed or covetousness. Money is good in the hand of a believer who sees it as the tool for the gospel, and he or she is committed to God (the Source) to advance His kingdom no matter what. That is why the devil will do anything to keep money away from you. He knows money in your hands is equal to souls in Heaven!

What I'm saying in essence is that God desires us to prosper because it empowers its church to better fulfill its purpose in the world. Reaching out to the world through publications, advertisements, television and radio programs costs lots of money. How would this be achieved without the prosperity of God's children? How do you send missionaries and charity workers to distant lands without financial prosperity? How do you send aids to people, including fellow Christians, in distress without money? How do you fund ministries and provide for the ministers of God?

That aside, just as the magnetism of the glory of God upon the prosperous Christian draws people to His God, so also does it happen to a prosperous church. People are naturally more easily drawn to success than failure; to comfort rather than discomfort. Imagine how easy it would be to invite someone to a church that is well-built and furnished, with functional ACs and electrifying sound systems. Imagine how long the invitee would want to stay in that church and how attentive he would be to the sermon. Now, compare that to a church in a ramshackle building, with leaking roof, suffocating heat and squeaking sound systems. The difference would be clear. And why shouldn't God want to prosper His people and His church to achieve this?

Of course, I'm not saying a church must be fully comfortable before it can function or that people should wait for comfort before attending a church; but we must know that aside from the human appeal, God Himself deserves and desires a befitting place of worship.

The prosperity of God's children, especially the ministers of God, also makes people to know that serving God does not automatically confer the yoke of poverty on you as many have been led to believe. God frowns at human employers oppressing or depriving their employees of legitimate rights. How could God be guilty of same? If God does not prosper those working for Him but consigns them to a life of penury and wretchedness, who would want to work for Him and who would see Him as a just God?

Really, we just have to begin to accept it that there is no reason why God would prefer us to be poor rather than being prosperous. We have come so far in Christianity and the revelation of the word of God is moving men and women of God into new horizon in the subject of prosperity. I think born again children of God must stop apologizing for being rich financially and living a better life, for it is in the light of their prosperity God is being glorified.

I remember that when I declared that God was calling me into ministry, I was just nineteen years old. My parents were so concerned about my welfare, as well as the "burden of poverty" that I would have to carry all my life. Their fear had been based on the stigma attached to all ministers of God that made them represent poverty. And some church congregants actually bought into the lie that you are destined for poverty all your life when you sign up to serve God in a full-time capacity. So they positioned themselves to make their pastors poorer in order to humble him.

As should be expected, we also saw decreases in response to the gospel in the past, since no one wanted to identify with a God who made His people poor. Now, we have a better understanding that Satan has succeeded enough in this area. This is the time for a turnaround as we look into the perfect law of liberty to claim our redemptive rights in Christ Jesus, financial prosperity included!

CHAPTER 4

PROVISIONS FOR YOUR PROSPERITY

"“Then He said to him, “A certain man gave a great supper and invited many, and sent his servant at supper time to say to those who were invited, ‘Come, for all things are now ready.”' (Luke 14:16).

Yes, all things are ready. This is even more interesting than all you've read so far. Not only does God want you to prosper but He has actually put everything in place to make your prosperity a reality. So, it's not as if you even have to struggle to make it work out – the provision is already made and bound with a seal of guarantee that can never fail! The question therefore is not whether God wants to prosper you or whether He has the power to do so but whether YOU want to enter into the realm of prosperity that God has graciously provided for you.

What are the provisions God has made to ensure that you spend every day of your life in prosperity?

THE ABRAHAMIC COVENANT

"Therefore know that only those who are of faith are sons of Abraham.And the Scripture, foreseeing that God would justify the Gentiles by faith, preached the gospel to Abraham beforehand, saying, "In you all the nations shall be blessed." So then those who are of faith are blessed with believing Abraham." (Galatians 3:7-9).

Hallelujah, this is glorious! Now prepare yourself for a repositioning into the realm of supernatural abundance. Guess what? The scripture says that if you're born again, not only do you become engrafted into the lineage of Abraham but you automatically become blessed as He was!

How is this possible? It's simply because of the undying power of the covenant of God with Abraham. It was a covenant of unlimited blessings to him and his descendants to come. Let me show you the components of the covenant – so you will know the riches of your heritage as a child of God and a descendant of Abraham. But first you must understand what a covenant is, so you can know how reliable and unchangeable your guarantee of prosperity is.

A covenant is a contract or agreement between two or more parties; or more precisely, it is a binding agreement between two or more parties with attendant conditionality. From the beginning of creation, God has continued to work on the basis of covenant. He had a covenant with Adam – to have him stay in the Garden of Eden continually and remain spiritually alive, as long as he did not eat the forbidden fruit. He had a covenant with Noah – that He would never again destroy the earth with a flood – the rainbow being its token. He had a covenant with Abraham (which I'll be explaining shortly). And He also had covenants with Moses, the Israelites, David and so on.

The unique thing about a covenant as you must have seen from the definition above is that it is BINDING once the conditions are met. Especially, if it's a covenant between God and man, you can be sure that God will NEVER fail, once an individual keeps to the terms. Once God swears a covenant, it is sealed and backed by His holiness – and regardless of the magnitude of the promises involved in it, He would ensure that He fulfills it all to the letter. This was why God declared concerning his covenant with David, "My covenant I will not break, Nor alter the word that has gone out of My lips. Once I have sworn by My holiness; I will not lie to David: His seed shall endure forever, And his throne as the sun before Me" (Psalms 89:34-36). Several years later, Jeremiah wrote: "Thus says the Lord: 'If you can break My covenant with the day and My covenant with the night, so that there will not be day and night in their season, then My covenant may also be broken with David My servant, so that he shall not have a son to reign on his throne…" (Jeremiah 33:20-21).

And concerning this Abrahamic covenant, of which we are partakers, the Scripture says, "For when God made a promise to Abraham, because He could swear by no one greater, He swore by Himself, saying, "Surely blessing I will bless you, and multiplying I will multiply you." And so, after he had patiently endured, he obtained the promise. For men indeed swear by the greater, and an oath for confirmation is for them an end of all dispute. Thus God, determining to show more abundantly to the heirs of promise the immutability of His counsel, confirmed it by an oath, that by two immutable things, in which it is impossible for God to lie, we might[b] have strong consolation, who have fled for refuge to lay hold of the hope set before us." (Hebrews 6:13-18).

I have given you the above preamble so you can understand how powerful and dependable the covenant provision God has made for your prosperity is. As a minister of God once said, "The covenant is so powerful that it has eternally committed God to your prosperity. It is one thing God cannot break. And that is to show you that if God cannot break the covenant of prosperity, no economic situation can do it. Global meltdown is no match. The covenant is your sure access to wealth and riches because no force in hell can handle the covenant."

So what is the Abrahamic covenant? It's here in Genesis 12:1-3: "Now the Lord had said to Abram: "Get out of your country, from your family and from your father's house, to a land that I will show you. I will make you a great nation; I will bless you and make your name great; and you shall be a blessing. I will bless those who bless you, and I will curse him who curses you; And in you all the families of the earth shall be blessed."

Abraham (then known as Abram) was to be greatly blessed and he was to be a channel of blessing to all who would tap into his covenant with God – only on one condition: he must disconnect and depart from his idolatrous background and dwell in another land where God would show him. Did he fulfill the condition? Certainly! Genesis 12:4 says, "So Abram departed as the Lord had spoken to him, and Lot went with him. And Abram was seventy-five years old when he departed from Haran."

Abraham fulfilled his own part of the covenant of blessing and you can trust God – He did exactly as He had said (I already showed you how Abraham was mightily blessed in chapter one). More importantly, God later re-established his covenant with Abraham and expanded the scope of the blessing in it to include all his descendants, including YOU! Genesis 17:3-7: "Then Abram fell on his face, and God talked with him, saying: "As for Me, behold, My covenant is with you, and you shall be a father of many nations. No longer shall your name be called Abram, but your name shall be Abraham; for I have made you a father of many nations. I will make you exceedingly fruitful; and I will make nations of you, and kings shall come from you. And I will establish My covenant between Me and you and your descendants after you in their generations, for an everlasting covenant, to be God to you and your descendants after you."

Of course, I don't need to remind you again of how much God blessed Abraham and in fulfillment of His covenant, His descendants. I showed you in chapter one how Isaac, the son of Abraham, was super-abundantly blessed and made prosperous. And Jacob, who was the son of Isaac too was mega-wealthy, including his twin-brother, Esau.

Indeed, the power of the covenant of prosperity upon Abraham was so strong that anyone connected to him, including those who were not his direct children, were blessed. For example, of Lot, his nephew, who lived and worked with him, the Scripture says, he became so prosperous that his employees and those of Abraham were competing for space to manage their resources. Genesis 13:5-7 says, "Lot also, who went with Abram, had flocks and herds and tents. Now the land was not able to support them, that they might dwell together, for their possessions were so great that they could not dwell together. And there was strife between the herdsmen of Abram's livestock and the herdsmen of Lot's livestock…"

Again, as I said before, the blessing of the covenant is unalterable. This was why even when Joseph, Jacob's son, was sold to slavery, the covenant continued to speak in His life. Slavery couldn't alter the plan of God for his lineage (Genesis 39:2-3). Gloriously enough, this is the same covenant you have been brought into through redemption in Christ Jesus. The covenant of everlasting abundance.

Let me show you the Scripture again, in case this sounds too good to be true. "Therefore know that only those who are of faith are sons of Abraham. And the Scripture, foreseeing that God would justify the Gentiles by faith, preached the gospel to Abraham beforehand, saying, "In you all the nations shall be blessed." So then those who are of faith are blessed with believing Abraham." (Galatians 3:7-9).

We are wrapped up into wealth by the covenant God made with Abraham. This covenant is an everlasting covenant. In other words, it is from generation to generation. Everyone connected with the Abrahamic covenant, including the nation of Israel, is connected to generational blessings.

The reason the Jewish people are so prosperous is because they understand the covenant of Abraham, as they are descendants of Abraham. They carry this mentality with them always. They believe that being blessed, which includes making money, is their birthright. Put them in the ghetto, and within a matter of weeks, months or years you will see them emerging as a formidable group to reckon with. They take the major part of the city. They are experts when it comes to the principles of business success. That's why you will never see a Jewish person on social welfare. Thousands of years after the Abrahamic covenant was established, it continues to work for them. And you as a believer in Jesus Christ have been wrapped into this covenant because you've become part of the Israel of God through the blood of Jesus!

THE REDEMPTIVE DEATH OF CHRIST

This is the most powerful provision that has sealed and guaranteed your prosperity in life. Not only did the death of Christ on the cross engraft you as a believer into the family line of Abraham to be a partaker of his blessing, but it has actually broken the power of poverty in your life.

A man of God once shared a revelation he had from God on this accomplishment of Christ. He said, "The Lord spoke to me and said, "Don't pray for money anymore. You have authority through my name to claim prosperity. I have already put gold, silver, and cattle on a thousand hills for my man Adam, and I gave him dominion over it. After he sold out to Satan, the second Adam, Jesus Christ, came to redeem you from the hand of the enemy and to remove you from the curse of the law. Now, instead of praying that I would do it, because I have made provision for your needs, all you need do is say, 'Satan, take your hands off my money.' Just claim what you need. You reign in life by Christ Jesus."

What a revelation! Indeed, part of the consequences of the sin of Adam was poverty. But Jesus came to destroy the curse released on Adam through the shedding of His blood on the Cross and to restore us back to the dignity we had lost. We are no longer under the curse of poverty.

As you accept Christ into your life, you are adopted into the family of God. Now you're a child of God. You are a joint heir with Christ. You are a rightful and natural partaker of the wealth of the Heavenly Father.

Our God will never run out of resources, including money. If you are His covenant child you deserve the best that God has to offer - just as you always want the best for your children. God owns all the resources of the earth and He has made them available for you through Jesus' blood. He will give you all you need in abundance.

Now, hear this: "For you know the grace of our Lord Jesus Christ, that though He was rich, yet for your sakes He became poor, that you through His poverty might become rich." (2 Corinthians 8:9). This scripture is the most powerful case ever for your dominion over poverty. Poverty is not permitted in the life of the believer because Christ paid the price. He became poor for my sake. To choose to remain in poverty is to make the sacrifice of Christ of no effect. He had us in mind while hanging on the cross. He paid the price on our behalf. He doesn't want us to preach the good news with a wretched lifestyle. The Kingdom of God is exalted above all kingdoms of the earth. Through His poverty we have been made rich. You are rich. Don't ever say you are poor. Declare it loud and clear, I AM RICH!

Apostle Paul in Philippians 4:19 said, "And my God shall supply all your need according to His riches in glory by Christ Jesus." Notice "in Christ Jesus." In Christ Jesus all things are provided and perfected. Your supply on earth depends on His riches in glory. He bore the curse on our behalf so you don't have to live under the curse again. The Scripture says in Galatians 3:13, "Christ has redeemed us from the curse of the law, having become a curse for us (for it is written, "Cursed is everyone who hangs on a tree"

In Jesus name, the curse of poverty is shattered in your life now! Don't celebrate poverty. Don't allow any religious error of "righteousness is synonymous with poverty" to overshadow your powerful covenant right in Christ. You are saved and freed from poverty through the redemptive work of Christ on the cross!

CHAPTER 5

ACTIVATE YOUR PROSPERITY!

Now that it has been established that you were created to be prosperous, destined to be prosperous, covenanted to be prosperous and that the provisions for your prosperity have been made, what's left for you to do?

It is to make the shift and WALK STRAIGHT INTO YOUR PROSPERITY!

How do you do this? You follow the divine principles that help to activate your prosperity. You see, God is a God of principle. And if you can abide by His principles, you will never know limitation. You will be celebrated on earth and in heaven.

When God blessed Abraham, He put forth His

principle that will activate and sustain the blessing. He told Abraham and his descendants after him to obey and keep his commandment. He said if they did, the covenant of blessings will remain with them. Abraham had to follow through the details of the covenant agreement so that the blessing could be transferred through generations after generations of the Israelite nation. God Himself testified of Abraham that he would command his family to follow Him (Genesis 18:19).

Get this straight then. In this kingdom of abundance and prosperity into which you have been brought, God is not a respecter of persons, but principles. You keep the rules and you get the goods.

So, what principles will unlock and sustain the overflow of prosperity into your life?

1. Establish a Solid Relationship with God

A genuine relationship with God is the first requirement for a prosperous life. So, do you have a relationship with God? Are you born again? The Bible says, "Nevertheless the solid foundation of God stands, having this seal: "The Lord knows those who are His," and, "Let everyone who names the name of Christ depart from iniquity." (2 Timothy 2:19). We cannot continue to sin and ask the grace of God to abound.

Prosperity is the product of God's grace reaching out to us in Christ Jesus.

Jesus is the source of life. Once you receive Christ into your life and your sins are forgiven, you will be accepted into God's beloved family. One interesting thing is that to be a part of God's family is easy. No matter how terrible your sin or life might have been, the blood on the cross is potent and powerful to cleanse you completely. Therefore, if you have not made any commitment to Christ before, do it now. There is abundant life in Christ that transcends prosperity. It is eternal life. Sin separates us from God, but Jesus paid the price so that we can be reconciled back to God and gain access to His grace and the manifold blessings He has in store for us.

If you have not been saved and you want to do so, please say this prayer:

Lord God, I thank you for the sacrifice of Christ on the cross for my sins. I thank you for the blood that was shed that I might be set free. I acknowledge that I am a sinner but I trust in the redemptive work of Christ for my salvation. Please forgive me my sins and wash me with the precious blood of Jesus. From today, I receive Jesus as my Savior and Lord. Help me to live for you all the days of my life. I ask this in Jesus' name.

I congratulate you, if you have sincerely said that prayer. You have been received into the family of God and positioned for abundant blessings. Your continued connection with God will make a difference in your quest for prosperity. If a tree is cut down from its source it will cease to flourish. It will dry up and die. So, you must maintain a good relationship with God always. Jesus must be the center of your life. Everything you do, say, think or aspire to be must be for the glory of God.

Once again, I say, settle you relationship with God first. You have the audacity to prosper when you grab the revelation of God's ownership of silver and gold. Pursue God and gold will not be your problem!

2. Live a Life of Daily Obedience to God

Your relationship with God is tested by your obedience to His word. Moses, through the Spirit of God, told the Israelites in Deuteronomy 28:1, "Now it shall come to pass, if you diligently obey the voice of the Lord your God, to observe carefully all His commandments which I command you today, that the Lord your God will set you high above all nations of the earth."

So, how do you respond when God speaks to you? This will significantly affect your quest for prosperity.

Jesus is not only your Savior, He is also your Lord! Thus, are you ready to say, "Yes, Lord" whenever He instructs you?

Job 36:11 reveals an instructive and very enlightening secret about the power of obedience in unlocking the door of prosperity: "If they obey and serve Him, They shall spend their days in prosperity, and their years in pleasures."

Our prosperity is in our obedience. If you are a parent, it is natural that you celebrate the child who obeys you on a regular basis. Your heart is refreshed when your child knows and obeys your instruction as you guide him through life. If we, earthly parents who are not perfect in nature ourselves, know the value of obedience and celebrate it in our children, how much more God! So, take His words seriously!

The passage above says that if you do obey God, you will spend your days in prosperity. God's instruction may sound foolish, or uncommon, but that is your ticket to prosperity. Develop genuine love for God and His Kingdom (Matthew 6:33). Spend quality time with God in worshipping, studying the word and praying.

As a pastor, I have seen that people draw near to God only when they are in financial crisis. Sadly, that is when they attend all mid-week services and pray the loudest. But where were they when things were going well? They were on their own and kept aloof from God. Suddenly, as crisis hits them from all corners, they start being on fire for God. Well, I'd say that it's okay that they're suddenly on fire for God, as long as they keep the fire burning and remain consistent in their obedience to God's word.

Nothing can dislocate you from the flow of financial success in life if you are connected with God through constant obedience. Obey him, worship Him, and be devoted to serve Him all your life and you will be a perpetual testimony of God's unceasing riches on earth.

3. Passionately Reject Poverty

Desire to prosper and be rich in life. Rouse yourself, get up from the "poverty land" and determine not to return there. Embrace prosperity as your birthright in Christ. Hate poverty with passion. Believe that the same God who redeemed you from your sin and shame is powerful enough to redeem you from you poverty, lack and want. I have shouted it in my teachings again and again, "You should not be broke one more day in your life!". God's reservoir doesn't run dry. This is your season to break the backbone of poverty in your life.

The verse in 3 John 2 that we read earlier emphasizes

something very important that I'd like to show you again. It says, "Beloved, I pray that you may prosper in all things and be in health, just as your soul prospers." John gave this charge to believers - that you may prosper in all things. ALL THINGS. Some believers believe in the salvation of their soul, which is good. Some believe in healing, which is fantastic! But what about ALL THINGS, including your finances?

Prosperity, as we saw in the first chapter, implies wellness in all things. God is an all-encompassing God. Jesus did not die for some part of your success in life; He died for all. He died for your sins and the consequences of your sins. He died for your sicknesses and diseases, as well as your poverty. So John says, "Just as YOUR SOUL PROSPERS"! – which means that every aspect of your life should be flourishing, just as your soul is doing. Your salvation is not maximized if you die broke!

Haggai 2:8 says, "'The silver is Mine, and the gold is Mine,' saith the LORD of hosts." So, contrary to the view of the world or even some Christians, God does not want His children to be poor, broke and dejected. He wants them to represent Him in wealth and resources. Like begets like. You have the DNA of financial prosperity. If your father is the owner of silver and gold (money) then you are the owner of silver and gold too. The father's inheritance naturally flows to the children.

Since I caught this revelation by the help of the Holy Spirit I have never seen myself broke again. Never! I walk around with a different mentality. I am not a poor man trying to get rich. I am a rich man living in the wealth created by the God of the universe (my Father). This is the same mentality you must have. I have known poverty; I have made up my mind not to return there again. I refuse to be poor again!

Hear what the Psalmist says of himself: "The LORD is my shepherd; I shall not want." (Psalms 23:1). He said this because, being a human shepherd himself, he knew that the shepherd always feeds the sheep with what he has. And knowing that the surest thing ever is that God has it all, he declared that there is no reason to lack since God is his shepherd. God will not withhold any good thing from the righteous. So if you are connected to God, you are connected to unlimited prosperity. Don't be ignorant of this fact. The enemy is taking advantage of Christians' ignorant on the covenant. Right from today, you shall not be in want in Jesus mighty name!

4. Position Yourself For Prosperity

To position yourself for prosperity, you must accept that believing God for abundant life is not a crime; it is laying hold of your covenant right as a child of God. This demands that you renew your mind with the word of God and allow the Holy Spirit to take you through the journey of change. Until then, you can be saved, speaking in tongues and attending all church services and still be poor and broke.

Let me use my story as an example. I was born into poverty. I know poverty firsthand. We were so poor that even the poor called us poor. I was so used to poverty that I often told my friends in school that I liked sleeping on bare floor than sleeping on mattress. And they would laugh at me. It was not my fault. By default, I was celebrating the life I only knew to be real to me.

Sadly, by the time I got saved, I was not anticipating that things would get better. The scriptures were misinterpreted to us. We had been told that we should not love the world or anything that is in the world. So I stayed out of anything having to do with money. It wasn't until I started studying my Bible and listening to messages from Bishop David Oyedepo, the presiding Bishop of Living Faith Church Worldwide, that I started to understand that I had been cheatimg and limiting myself. Pastor Oyedepo would shout it that "God's will is to prosper you! He gives you power to get wealth."

Surely faith comes by hearing and hearing by the word of God. After listening to him, I would pray and ask God to prosper me. Then I started asking some questions. One of them was, if I am a child of God, why am I still poor when the Bible says I ought to prosper?

I believe that if you know how to ask good questions, you will know how to get good answers! The first and most powerful insight that I got was that wealth belongs to God. This implies that wealth comes from Him. All good and perfect gifts are from God (James 1:17) and He gives the power to get wealth (Deuteronomy 8:18).

Let me assure you. The fact that you have not become prosperous does not mean that God is incapable of transforming your condition. You have been given all things that pertain to life and godliness - including finances – in Christ Jesus. However, if you are not properly positioned in your mind, you may miss out of the wealth due to you.

5. Settle the Issue of Pride

God warned the Israelite a lot about this subject, especially when it has to do with His blessing on their lives. He cautioned them on the possibility of taking credit for their wealth and eventually forgetting Him. An elaborate warning on this is contained in Deuteronomy 28:12-18. But let me just quote the last verse here: "And you shall remember the LORD your God, for it is He who gives you power to get wealth, that He may establish His covenant which He swore to your fathers, as it is this day."

Believe it or not, if God talked about it then it must be taken seriously. God resists the proud and gives grace to the humble. Humility is the ticket to your financial promotion in life. Humble yourself before God and He will lift you up. In God's Kingdom, the prerequisite for promotion is not arrogance, but humility. Wealth without humility equals destruction. God loves you and so He will not give you something that will destroy you. He will give you enough that you can handle. However, it is your responsibility to build yourself up in godly character; growing in the fruit of the Spirit. This is not just because you want to enjoy more wealth per se but because you want to enjoy the abundant life Jesus has purchased for you on the Cross.

6. Take Tithing Seriously

When you get saved, your first responsibility is to support your local church with tithes and offering. I was nineteen years old when my pastor introduced me to tithing from the Bible. I have not forgotten the scenario. It was summer of 1996 when we met at the supermarket. After normal exchange of greetings and pleasantries, he asked me if I gave my tithe to the Church. As innocent as I was, I told him I did not understand what tithing was all about. Today, I am ever grateful for the seed he sowed into my life. Today, I have seen God move in extraordinary ways in my finances as a result of my obedience to tithing.

Malachi 3:10 says, "Bring all the tithes into the storehouse, That there may be food in My house, And try Me now in this," Says the Lord of hosts, "If I will not open for you the windows of heaven And pour out for you such blessing That there will not be room enough to receive it."

Tithing is the token of God's covenant for financial release. We are covenant people. For the covenant to work we must be committed to working it. Tithe means one-tenth or ten percent. This is God's. In actual fact, the entire hundred percent of your income belongs to God. However, God is only requesting for a mere ten percent of it. The implication is that you are placing something on the altar of God for your financial breakthrough. You are inviting God into your finances. Most importantly, you are worshipping God with your substance and the first fruit of your increase. What you are saying in essence is that God is your financial source.

Disobedience to the Biblical principle of tithing limits your access to the covenant wealth. Of course, you will make it to heaven, but you will discover how much of God's grace and blessings you have missed on earth when you get there. If you are a pastor, the financial prosperity of your church depends on the percentage of people who tithe. The church cannot grow financially beyond the tithes. I have seen it. When I taught about tithing, the vast majority of people who started tithing exploded financially. Not only that, their lives and livelihoods improved significantly and they started enjoying a stressed-free life.

Tithing affects all aspects of your life. Your tithe represents you in the presence of God. When people who are in financial crisis come to me, after settling the issue of their relationship with God, the next approach is to settle the issue of tithing. I call tithe the key to the door of financial powerhouse of heaven.

Here are the three ways to tithe for result:

- **Tithe consistently** – Don't miss giving your tithe when it is due to do so. Don't use your tithe for something else. It is not part of your budget; it's God's.

- **Tithe correctly** – Tithe is defined as 10% of all your income, not less.

- **Tithe cheerfully** – Be excited for the opportunity to give to the Gospel. God loves cheerful givers. It is better not to give, than giving with bitterness.

7. Make Yourself Trustworthy to God

God is looking for trustees of His wealth. One of the greatest and honest questions to ask yourself as a child of God is, can God trust me? Your access to the wealth God has for you will depend on how you answer this critical question of trust. As the Scripture affirms, to whom much is given much is expected.

God knows the intent of your heart. Why do you want money? A Christian brother was asked, "If God gives you ten million dollars, what would you do with it?" He was silent for a while, then when he finally answered, he said, "I will put the money in the bank, resign from my current job, pay off my house, buy luxury cars, and go on a vacation!" Did you see that? Nothing about the Kingdom! This is why many

Christians are broke. They have not answered the question of trust.

To be trustworthy to God in terms of financial prosperity, there must be kingdom understanding of money, as well as the discipline to manage God's resources. God does not waste His resources. Money in the kingdom is not for self-gratification, or selfish ambition. Trust me, money is a powerful force, and can be dangerous if it falls into the hand of an immature, greedy, and wicked person. God judges and responds to the intent of people's heart. So, ask yourself why do you want money? How do you spend the little God has committed to you hands now?

Are you a good steward of God's resources? Check your spending habit. Also examine your motives. If you are faithful in handling few things, He will commit more into your hands. Matthew 25:23: "His lord said to him, 'Well done, good and faithful servant; you were faithful over a few things, I will make you ruler over many things. Enter into the joy of your lord.'"

Many of us want to be millionaires overnight. We want to skip the process of trust. But before God can entrust a million into your hand he would have tested your heart and proven that you are well-positioned for it and can manage it well for His own glory.

Money in itself is not evil, but it is the heart of those who handle money that is evil. In 1999, the Church I attended in Nigeria was involved in a building project. However, the project was going to be abandoned because of lack of finance. The Church began to pray for divine intervention. Not too long, a man joined the Church, and told us God sent him to build the Church in 52 days. He was bold with his announcement to us so much that most of us were shocked. As a volunteer worker then, I thought, "where is he going to get the money? Some other people were speculating, is this man genuine?" It is amazing that sometimes we pray and when the answer arrives we couldn't recognize it.

However, we saw God moved through this man and the building project was completed in 52 days. He told us he had made covenant with God, that whatever He asked him to do with his money he would not hesitate. "The money belongs to God, I am just the earthly custodian," he said. That blew most of us away. He is a very humble man who has dedicated his life and resources to God's cause. God trusted and committed lots of money into his hands.

8. Settle the Issue of Diligence

Diligence is the bedrock of prosperity. There is no substitute for hard work. Prayer is great, but cannot do for you what hard work is designed to do. As a matter of fact one practical way to walk out of poverty to a lifestyle of wealth is through hard work. Laziness is the surest path to poverty. The book of proverbs presents this truth clearly without mincing words:

"He who has a slack hand becomes poor, But the hand of the diligent makes rich" (Proverbs 10:4)

A lazy man or woman has no future. A lazy person will blame everything, everyone, including the government for his or her poverty. Stop the blame game; find something to do and pour your passion into it and grace will be release on you. I often say that, God only promises to bless the work of your hand (Deuteronomy 28:12). If you do not put your hands to work there is nothing God will bless.

Hard work will distinguish you and set you above your contemporaries. Be diligent in business; See God work wonders in your life!

9. Think Beyond Your Wages

Sometimes, the problem is that many Christians have tied their prosperity to their paychecks. Their financial vision has not exceeded the figure of their weekly or biweekly paycheck. They have no clue that their prosperity does not depend on how much they earn weekly or biweekly, but on the supernatural blessing from above.

If you tie your prosperity to your wages, you are limited. As a kingdom citizen your economy does not depend on the system of this world, but on the system of heaven, the invisible world. Therefore, you must transcend the natural mindset; look beyond the current balance in your bank account, see a different bank where everything is available. All the money you need to operate here on earth to glorify God in the process is available in the heavenly account. I live with this sense of confidence all the time. The Father's resources are always available in abundant supply for your provisions. That is why you cannot be broke anymore!

10. Pray For Prosperity

"Save now, I pray, O LORD; O LORD, I pray, send now prosperity" (Psalm 118:12)

Prosperity is a choice. Many Christians because of faulty teachings on wealth think it's weird to pray for money. They find it even uncomfortable when a minister talks about money in the Church. They always have the notion that the minister is there to take their money, and if you preach about it or ask people to pray about it, it becomes absurd.

Get comfortable with wealth if you must experience financial prosperity. Don't be ashamed to ask God for money. God is not embarrassed, so why are you? The Bible tells us that we have not because we ask not. And our prayer has to be specific - Money.

Because some Christians are not comfortable to mention money in their prayer they simply say, "God bless me." As pastor, occasionally I ask our congregation to write out their prayer requests so I can pray on them in my private prayer. I like to read through all the prayer requests. 85% of the prayers are not specific. People who need money are asking me to agree for God to bless them, and enlarge them. "God bless me" - with what? If you want money ask for money, just as you will ask for healing when you are sick. God is not embarrassed!

I am always amazed by the grace of God. One day I was in need of money to help my younger sister with her tuition in Nigeria as she going back to School. She had saved some money toward her tuition, but she always needed extra to make up the balance. It was so weird that I didn't have the amount she was asking for at the time. She needed the money on a Tuesday or else the registration would be closed.

On Sunday morning at about 1:30am God spoke to

me about seed-faith, and instructed me to sow seed during service in the Church. I did as I was instructed. Getting home that Sunday, I prayed for money just as I would pray passionately for anything I believe God for. The following day someone sent me a text message that God had placed it in her heart to give me some money, that she wanted to know how to fulfilled it. I quickly texted my account number to her. It was not long when I checked my bank account and found that she had deposited the exact amount I needed for my sister's tuition. Ask God for money. Be specific when you ask.

"Ask, and it will be given to you; seek, and you will find; knock, and it will be opened to you. For everyone who asks receives, and he who seeks finds, and to him who knocks it will be opened. Or what man is there among you who, if his son asks for bread, will give him a stone? Or if he asks for a fish, will he give him a serpent?" (Matthew 7:7-10)

As long as you live on this planet and you want to fulfill God's mandate for your life you will be in need of money. "Lord, send now prosperity" - that is the specific prayer. But if you are contented with what you have, then it may not be necessary because you don't need lots of money to take care of yourself. However, If you want the Gospel of our Lord Jesus Christ to be preached, help your family, and lots of people to succeed in life, then you will need to pray for God to put more money in your hands.

11. Break Off the Yoke of Poverty

This final principle is deliberately placed last because it doesn't always apply to everyone. However, it is an important principle because one of the reasons many have accepted the lie that they're destined to be poor in life is their repeated inability to break through in the area of prosperity. Despite several attempts and even application of several principles and formulas as mentioned above, they seem to always encounter brick walls, failures and frustrations. And so they conclude, with the aid of some ignorant preachers and misapplied scriptures, that it is their portion to be poor in life.

What many in this category do not know is that it is neither God nor "destiny" that is keeping them bound to poverty. It is the yoke of the enemy upon their lives, which could sometimes be traced to their family line or some other satanic sources. So, if it appears you are in this category, then you must be ready to violently battle the enemy with the weapons that God has provided for you. "For the weapons of our warfare are not carnal but they are mighty through God, pulling down strongholds…" (2 Corinthians 10:4-5).

Yes, you must vehemently deploy the weapons of warfare including prayer and fasting, application of the blood of Jesus and pronouncements of faith to pull down every stronghold of poverty, nullify every handwriting and covenant of wretchedness and cancel every negative pronouncements of misery upon your life and destiny. That was the important step that Jabez took – otherwise, he might have spent his entire life in sorrow and wretchedness. (1 Chronicles 4:9-10)

But it was not only Jabez that had to contend before having the will of God fulfilled in his life in the area of prosperity. Even Isaac, who was a son of promise, had to labor to reverse the works of the enemies in his life after they went to had blocked all the wells his father had left for him (Genesis 26:15-22). Jacob who later became Israel had to contend with the schemes of Laban who wanted to make him remain a servant for life – in fact he had to break free by force! (Genesis 31). Thank God that none of these people regarded limitation and poverty as God's will for their lives!

CHAPTER 6

EMPOWERMENT FOR PROSPERITY

"And you shall remember the Lord your God, for it is He who gives you power to get wealth, that He may establish His covenant which He swore to your fathers, as it is this day" (Deuteronomy 8:18).

This is an extraordinary dimension of revelation on the subject of financial and material prosperity. Long before all the various campaigns by governments, institutions and socio-economic experts in nations of the world on the necessity of empowering peoples and communities, God had originated the concept and made it clear that one of His key specialties is EMPOWERING and EQUIPPING His children with all that they need to succeed, to prosper and to prevail in life.

God made this great revelation to the Israelites – and by extension, anyone who believes he is an Israelite of God today – for two reasons. The first is to assure us to depend on Him as the source of all that we need for breakthrough, prosperity and wealth; and the second is to admonish us to continually acknowledge and appreciate Him all the days of our lives for all that we may possess.

POWER TO GET WEALTH DEFINED!

So what does God mean when He says He gives power to get wealth? Or rather what does this power to get wealth mean for you as a believer?

1. **It is the skills, strength, inspiration and insight to acquire wealth.** God can so bless you with natural gifts or even spontaneous ideas and inspirations that instantly transform you into a wealth-creating machine. Proverbs 18:16 says, "A man's gift makes room for him, and brings him before great men." Look around you and think of all the great and reputable names that are flourishing in business, industry, arts, literature, science and technology - and you'll discover the manifold power of wealth-creating skills, inspiration and ideas. Most of these people seem to possess such capacity to generate wealth with ease.

Have you ever wondered where they get their brilliant ideas and acumens from?

Interestingly some of these people do not even have the Holy Spirit in them and yet they are able to generate great ideas that generate legitimate wealth for them. How is this possible? The answer is clear: "Every good gift and every perfect gift is from above, and comes down from the Father of lights, with whom there is no variation or shadow of turning" (James 1:17).

This should challenge you as a Spirit-filled believer, who is LOADED with the creative power of God in his life. Because you belong to God, you have what it takes to become the next great thing in this generation. All you need to do is begin to activate and appropriate all the riches of wisdom and ideas from your Father into your life and you'll find yourself being supernaturally empowered for prosperity.

God blessed Isaac, Jacob, Joseph, David, Daniel and so many others in the scripture with special ideas, wisdom and skills to transform themselves into successful, prosperous and eminent men in their generations. Of a man called Bezaleel in particular, God emphatically said to Moses: "See, I have called by name Bezalel the son of Uri, the son of Hur, of the tribe of Judah. And I have filled him with the Spirit of God, in wisdom, in understanding, in knowledge, and in all manner of workmanship, to design artistic works, to work in gold, in silver, in bronze, in cutting jewels for setting, in carving wood, and to work in all manner of workmanship" (Exodus 31:2-5).

This is a graphic example of mental and creative empowerment from God – and I decree same into your life today in Jesus name!

2. **It is the enabling environment for wealth or the ability to arrive at your wealthy place!** If you observe closely, you'll notice that two ideas are rolled into one here - so, let me break it down for you. God can empower you for wealth by either leading you to an environment that will be so favorable to your flourishing, an environment full of open doors for your financial breakthrough; or He could supernaturally enrich your present environment so that doors that seemed to be locked suddenly begin to open, even without much effort on your part.

Let me show you examples of each of these scenarios from the scriptures. First, you have God telling the children of Israel that He was leading them "into a good land, a land of brooks of water, of fountains and depths that spring out of valleys and hills; A land of wheat, and barley, and vines, and fig trees, and pomegranates; a land of oil olive, and honey; A land wherein thou shalt eat bread without scarceness, thou shalt not lack any thing in it…" (Deuteronomy 8:7-9, KJV). Who blessed this land with all the riches and resources which the Israelites were to enjoy? It was God Himself and He chose to lead them there. They didn't know anything about the place. He was the one who specially created and prepared the place for their inheritance. And the Lord is still in the same business of doing same today.

Even the Psalmist testified, "The Lord is my shepherd; I shall not want. He maketh me to lie down in green pastures…" (Psalm 23:1-2). And at another time, he said, "…We went through fire and through water: but thou broughtest us out into a wealthy place" (Psalm 66:12). In both passages, the Psalmist's message is clear; it's God doing the leading into green pastures and a wealthy place. It's not about running here and there, searching for green pastures – let God empower and guide you to locate your green pastures!

The second part that I said I would show you is supernatural enrichment of your present location. You find a good example of that in the case of Isaac who dwelt in a land ravaged by famine and was thinking of relocating. But God told him to remain, with a promise to bless him – and He did exactly that. The blessing that Isaac eventually got from that same land was supremely bountiful (Genesis 26). You also find a good example in the case of Peter and the other disciples who had toiled all night without catching a fish. And yet, with the empowerment of the Spirit of God, they caught multitudes of fishes around the same spot (Luke 5:4-6).

3. **It is the connection and opportunity to make wealth.** Lots of people have talents, potentials, strengths and skills today but without the right connection and opportunity to showcase their skills and get recognized. Indeed, "the race is not to the swift, nor the battle to the strong, neither yet bread to the wise, nor yet riches to men of understanding, nor yet favour to men of skill; but time and chance happeneth to them." This is where divine empowerment is really paramount. God can connect you to the right helpers at the right time. He can make you to be at the right place at the right time where your skill is all that's needed to turn things around. He can push you to make the right investment that will forever yield bountiful rewards for you – just as Isaac sowed and reaped a hundredfold.

I can't count how many stories of people whose destinies have been changed and who have become millionaires and billionaires by circumstances that they themselves know are beyond their comprehension! I call that the grace to have access to financial abundance. Every child of God is rich but not all children of God have access. When you have that grace, the wealth of the Gentiles will locate you. When you have access, the treasures of darkness will begin to pour in your direction. When you have access, the call for financial opportunities will not stop coming. Shout ACCESS!!

4. **It is the ability to break through financial hardship and financial barriers to launch into financial abundance.** In other words, it is the ability to be immune to prevailing hardships and economic downturns. It's a special divine fortification to succeed where others are failing. It's a spirit of favor and excellence that makes one flourish in every situation and environment while others are complaining of famine. It is the perpetual mark of excellence and abundance that makes one successful and prosperous, whether in the prison or the palace, whether in a familiar or an unfamiliar territory.

Indeed, power to get wealth is more than earning income. It is about abundance! Until we all get to the point where we are not struggling to survive but have more than enough then we are not yet there. Until we break through financial scarcity, we are not yet there. Until we stop having to be thinking of how to pay our bills we are not yet there. Until we see that we have more in reserve to do the will of God we are not yet there. But God is taking us there! We are breaking barriers, limitations and forces stopping us by the power of the Holy Spirit in Jesus name.

5. **It is the capacity to sustain wealth**. God gives you power to get wealth by enlarging your capacity to manage and sustain the wealth. Not everybody can acquire wealth and sustain it. This is why God blesses us with wealth according to our individual capacities! (See the Parable of the Talents in Matthew 25). Many people are unaware of this secret. This is why they sometimes pray the wrong prayer - asking God for money, rather than asking Him to increase or enlarge their coast or capacity to create and sustain wealth. Jesus, for example, told His disciples in John 16:12-13: "I still have many things to say to you, but you cannot bear them now. However, when He, the Spirit of truth, has come, He will guide you into all truth…"

Did you see that? Many things He could have poured into their lives spiritually – but as at then, their capacity to receive, retain and maximize what He was willing to bless them with was limited. This was why He promised to deal with the limitation by sending the Holy Spirit upon them. The same thing happens physically and especially in your finances. God will not give you what will destroy you. If it is a fish you need,

He won't give you what will constitute a serpent to you. He will not give you what is beyond your power to manage. In fact, He said it clearly in Mark 2:22, "And no one puts new wine into old wineskins; or else the new wine bursts the wineskins, the wine is spilled, and the wineskins are ruined. But new wine must be put into new wineskins."

You're like the wineskin. And God will not give you what will break or overwhelm you. So, for you to continually receive His abundance, your coast and capacity must continue to be expanded – which, thankfully, God is able to work out, as it is a crucial part of the power He provides for us to make wealth! You know, there is what is called a "wealth thermostat". Donald Trump, for instance, has his thermostat set at a billion dollars. To be a billionaire means that your financial thermostat is at billion-dollar capacity. You have the capacity to create billions of dollars. If someone with a billion dollar capacity falls to a million-dollar capacity, that person is broke. So, in order to create wealth, God will first increase your capacity for the amount of wealth you desire.

6. It is the divine ability to multiply resources. Exponential multiplication is another means by which God demonstrates His power to get wealth to His children. With the release of this power on a business, venture or enterprise, it begins to grow and increase in leaps and bounds. Even if the enterprise had been at the point of death, God can release the power to get wealth, which will quicken, rejuvenate and catapult such venture to the peak of success and profitability. This has nothing to do with the intelligence or ingenuity of the owner. It's just the blessing of God at work.

A classic example of this was the case of the widow that needed money urgently in 2 Kings 4 to pay back the heavy debt her husband had incurred before his death. Even though the story clearly demonstrates the necessity of capacity enlargement - because the miraculous flow of oil from the only jar of oil she possessed never ceased until there was no more jar to be filled - it also demonstrates the divine power to generate wealth through multiplication of resources. This same power is available for you today. It will ensure that multiple-fold abundance backs up every little effort or investment you make. You continue to experience and enjoy extraordinary and EXPONENTIAL increase beyond your imaginations!

A CALL TO REMEMBRANCE

Now, I need to call your attention to what our introductory verse says again. It says, "and you shall remember the Lord your God, for it is He who gives you power to get wealth…" Two things must be noted here – and they are meant to be on your mind both before and after getting wealth.

First, before getting wealth, God expects you to remember that it is He alone who can give true, lasting and satisfying wealth. As Proverbs 10:22 says, "The blessing of the Lord makes one rich, and He adds no sorrow with it." Prosperity is not obtained by excessive struggling or through dubious means. You mustn't make getting wealth a do-or-die affair to the detriment of your soul.

Don't jeopardize your life, faith, health or family because of the pursuit of wealth. "For what profit is it to a man if he gains the whole world, and loses his own soul?" (Matthew 16:26). All you need do to be prosperous is follow the principles listed earlier in this book and then let the blessings of God naturally come upon you - and it shall be so.

Now, after getting wealth, you must also remember God by honoring Him with your life and resources. Draw closer to God with your life and continually promote the expansion of His Kingdom. Also, ensure to bless other people around you through godly use of your wealth.

Don't get carried away with pride, greed or selfishness! Remember, it's very good to have wealth but wealth must NEVER have you! The more you use your God-given wealth for the glory of God and the benefit of your fellow men, the more the blessing of God will continue to flow into your life.

CHAPTER 7

PROPHETIC PRAYER FOR PROSPERITY

As I have variously emphasized in this book, prosperity is part of a believer's Kingdom rights, which means it is one of the things he can legitimately pray for and get the attention of Heaven. In fact, Jesus categorically says in John 14:14, "If you ask anything in My name, I will do it." "Anything" here includes prosperity.

Just as David prayed to God to send prosperity, we can do likewise. David said, "Save now, I pray, O Lord; O Lord, I pray, send now prosperity (Psalms 118:25). We must not leave any stone unturned. It is time to pray, "Send now prosperity." Heaven is ready to answer.

Your days of poverty and scarcity are over in Jesus

name. I see you moving from the realm of "not enough" to the realm of "more than enough" in Jesus name! You have a covenant of provision in God. You must claim it through prayer.

Meditate on the following scriptures so that you can be stirred up to claim what rightly belongs to you.

- You shall eat in plenty and be satisfied, And praise the name of the LORD your God, Who has dealt wondrously with you; And My people shall never be put to shame (Joel 2:26).
- I have been young, and now am old; Yet I have not seen the righteous forsaken, Nor his descendants begging bread (Psalms 37:25).
- And my God shall supply all your need according to His riches in glory by Christ Jesus (Philippians 4:19).

DAY 1

Word Weapon: **2 Corinthians 8:9,** "For you know the grace of our Lord Jesus Christ, that though He was rich, yet for your sakes He became poor, that you through His poverty might become rich."

1. Father, thank you for providing for all my needs

according to your riches in glory through Christ in Jesus name.

2. Father, have mercy upon me, forgive me of all my sins and wash me in the blood of the Lamb in Jesus name.

3. Father, manifest Yourself in my life and finances today in Jesus name.

4. Father, by the power of the Holy Spirit, I destroy the curse of poverty and lack in my life in Jesus name.

5. Father, I decree that money will not be my master because I am made to rule over it, money is made to serve me. Therefore, Lord, send money to serve all my needs in Jesus name.

6. Father, open doors of great jobs and unlimited financial opportunities for my spouse and me in Jesus name.

7. Father, give me a stable and uninterrupted financial flow this year in Jesus name.

8. Father, I arrest every spirit of poverty and lack in my life and I declare that I shall not toil any more to survive in Jesus name.

9. Father, Your Word says, Jesus became poor that I might be rich. Therefore, I destroy every hindrance to my financial prosperity in Jesus name.

10. Father, release the abundance of heaven towards my direction and open up the treasures of the earth in my favor this year in Jesus name.

11. Father, give me the grace to be obedient to your Word in the area of tithing and giving of offerings towards Your kingdom in Jesus name.

12. Father, this is not my final destination; increase me drastically this year in Jesus name.

13. Father, have mercy upon me and paralyze the hands of the enemy over my finances in Jesus name.

14. Thank you Lord for answering my prayer in Jesus name. Amen!

DAY 2

Word Weapon: **2 Corinthians 9:8** And God is able to make all grace abound toward you, that you, always having all sufficiency in all things, may have an abundance for every good work.

1. Father, thank You for another day of prayer and for the grace to stand before Your throne. Be exalted in Jesus name.

2. Father, let me gain access to my wealthy place today and let all my prayers receive speedy responses from heaven in Jesus name.

3. Father, Your word says, I will eat in plenty and I shall not be ashamed. Therefore, destroy every garment of lack, shame and reproach that poverty brought upon me in Jesus name.

4. Father, unlock the heavens to release supernatural financial blessings to my destiny in Jesus name.

5. Father, I command the treasure of the hidden places to be transferred into my dwelling place in Jesus name.

6. God of abundance, let the land yield abundant prosperity for me and let the work of my hands be blessed with supernatural harvest in Jesus name.

7. Father, give me the power to get wealth for your kingdom sake and empower me with financial

ideas, insight and wisdom for kingdom expansion in Jesus name.

8. Lord, silver and gold belong to You, make your Church the evidence and the showcase of Your prosperity in Jesus name.

9. Father Lord, eliminate the ignorance that has kept me in perpetual poverty in Jesus name.

10. I declare that I shall lend to nations and I shall not borrow; I shall not beg from my enemies in Jesus name.

11. Father, deal with all spiritual wasters, and devourers of my finances and kill every spirit of financial misfortune in my life in Jesus name.

12. Father, today I breakthrough from every financial restriction placed upon me by the devil or his agents in Jesus name.

13. Father, let my cup overflow; give me more than enough and make me a blessing to nations in Jesus name.

14. Thank you Lord for answering my prayer in Jesus name. Amen!

DAY 3

Word Weapon: **Deuteronomy 8:18** And you shall remember the Lord your God, for it is He who gives you power to get wealth, that He may establish His covenant which He swore to your fathers, as it is this day.

1. Father, this is the day that You have made and I will rejoice and be glad in it in Jesus name.

2. Lord, today let my prayer come to You like a sweet smelling aroma in Jesus name.

3. Father, have mercy upon me and provide all my needs according to Your riches in glory in Jesus name.

4. Lord, Your word says, "The blessing of the Lord makes rich and add no sorrow with it." Therefore, Father, give me wealth with abundant peace, joy and health in Jesus name.

5. I receive the grace to overcome greed in my life in Jesus name.

6. I decree that my life, family, career and ministry will not experience lack or be broke any longer in Jesus name.

7. I curse the spirit of scarcity and economic break down and recession in my life in Jesus name.

8. I declare that I shall eat in plenty and be satisfied in Jesus name.

9. Lord, let all my seed of faith, prophetic offerings, and tithes yield extraordinary harvest in Jesus name.

10. Father, let every strange and satanic hand released to pull me down financially be paralyzed in Jesus name.

11. Father, by your mercy, correct every stupid and foolish decision that have drained my financial opportunities in Jesus name.

12. I command everything the enemy has planted or designed to reduce me financially to get out of my life, family and career now in Jesus name.

13. I receive showers of unlimited blessings in my life and the wisdom to manage and multiply the resources You have given me in Jesus name.

14. Thank you Lord for answering my prayers in Jesus name. Amen!

THE GREATEST PRAYER OF A LIFETIME

The greatest prayer of a lifetime is to be reconnected back to God in a living relationship. Relationship is the basis for asking. You cannot pray to a God whom you don't know and who does not know you. God wants to be intimate with you. This type of relationship is available to each one of us when we sincerely repent of our sins, ask for God's forgiveness, and receive His Son, Jesus, as our personal Lord and Savior. If you have never surrendered your life to God, or if you have turned away from God and you want to return to Him, now is the time. God is waiting for you. His arms are open wide to receive you. Just pray this simple prayer right now:

O Lord, be merciful to me, a sinner. I realize that I am a sinner. I need a Savior and you are my savior. I repent of every sin, every wrongdoing, and I ask for your forgiveness. I receive Jesus Christ, Your only begotten Son, as my Lord and my Savior. I believe that Jesus went to the cross for me and paid the price for my salvation, and now I receive Him into my heart. I declare that I am born again. I am a child of God. Old sins are gone, and I have a brand-new life in Christ in Jesus' name. Amen.

ABOUT PASTOR GBENGA SHOWUNMI

Pastor Gbenga Showunmi is an insightful speaker, serial entrepreneur, fearless visionary and apostolic leader.

A graduate of Oral Robert University, Tulsa, Oklahoma, from where he obtained a Master of Divinity degree, Pastor Gbenga is the Founder of Destinystar Ministries International, as well as being CEO of Cornerstone Creativity Group LLC and Cornerstone Publishing.

He is a well-travelled and sought-after speaker for conferences across the globe. His passion is to move people from where they are to where they ought to be in God's purposes and agenda for their lives.

Pastor Gbenga is the bestselling author of Moving Forward in the Storm, Your Supernatural Inheritance, Prophetic Prayer for Divine Intervention and Prophetic Prayer for Claiming Your Covenant Right.

He is married to his best friend, Pastor Victoria Showunmi, and they are blessed with three destiny children.

BOOKS BY PASTOR GBENGA SHOWUNMI

IN PURSUIT OF GREATNESS

In Pursuit of Greatness is the newest book by Pastor Gbenga Showunmi. This book presents practical insights on how you can step into your destiny and find fulfilment in life!

THE PROSPERITY MINDSET

The Prosperity Mindset is a revolutionary call to all believers to wake up from our self-inflicted slumber of substandard living and embrace the full package of glorious benefits that Christ has purchased for us with His blood. Properity belongs to us!

MOVING FORWARD IN THE STORM

In **Moving Forward in the Storm** Pastor Showunmi uses his own life experiences and lessons to help you rise above life's challenges. No matter how difficult the situation is, you have the capacity to prevail.

BOOKS BY PASTOR GBENGA SHOWUNMI

YOUR SUPERNATURAL INHERITANCE

In **Your Supernatural Inheritance** Pastor Gbenga Showunmi presents the idea that you are born into God's supernatural family and hence have extraordinary possessions that must be strategically located and possesed!

PROPHETIC PRAYER FOR DIVINE INTERVENTION

Prophetic Prayer for Divine Intervention is a collection of 21 Days prayer nuggets that will change your destiny. Diverse testimonies of miracles and breakthrough aboundfor those who have used this book.

PROPHETIC PRAYER FOR CLAIMING YOUR COVENANT RIGHTS

Prophetic Prayer for Claiming Your Covenant Rights is a 21 days prayer declarations that will turn your life around. There are 7 categories of covenant rights to lay claim of. Discover them in this book.

Made in the USA
Monee, IL
04 November 2026

67380793R00066